Take a Stand Against Bullying
SOCIAL BULLYING

Margaret Webb

Crabtree Publishing Company
www.crabtreebooks.com

Author: Maragaret Webb

Publishing plan research and development:
Sean Charlebois, Reagan Miller
Crabtree Publishing Company

Project coordinator: Kathy Middleton

Editorial director: Melissa McClellan

Art director: Tibor Choleva

Fictional Introductions: Maragaret Webb

Editors: Kristine Thornley, Rachel Stuckey, Molly Aloian

Proofreader: Kelly McNiven

Production coordinator: Margaret Amy Salter

Prepress technician: Margaret Amy Salter

Print coordinator: Katherine Berti

Developed and produced by: BlueApple *Works* Inc.

Consultants:
Adina Herbert, MSW, RSW
Social Worker, Youth Addictions and Concurrent Disorders Service
Centre for Addiction and Mental Health, Toronto, ON, Canada

Lesley Cunningham MSW, RSW
Social Worker - Violence Prevention

Photographs: Front cover: Shutterstock (all except bottom left), Thinkstock (bottom left); Title page, © littleny/ Shutterstock Inc.; contents: © Diego Cervo/ Shutterstock Inc.; p.4 © @erics/ Shutterstock Inc.; p.6 © Galina Barskaya/ Shutterstock Inc.; p.7 © Mandy Godbehear/ Shutterstock Inc.; p.8 © wrangler/ Shutterstock Inc.; p.9 © Paul Matthew Photography/ Shutterstock Inc.; p.10 © Andy Dean Photography/ Shutterstock Inc.; p.11 © Elena Elisseeva/ Shutterstock Inc.; p. 12 © Beth Van Trees/ Shutterstock Inc.; p. 15 © Tubol Evgeniya/ Shutterstock Inc.; p.16 © Helder Almeida/ Shutterstock Inc.; p.17, 27 © Monkey Business Images/ Shutterstock Inc.; p.18 © Creatista/ Shutterstock Inc.; p.19 © andrea michele piacquadio/ Shutterstock Inc.; p.20 © Gemenacom/ Shutterstock Inc.; p.21 © Christy Thompson/ Shutterstock Inc.; p.22 © Vanessa Nel/ Shutterstock Inc.; p.23 © GVictoria/ Shutterstock Inc.; p.24 © Aleshyn_Andrei/ Shutterstock Inc.; p.25 © Michel Borges / Shutterstock Inc.; p.26 © krivenko/ Shutterstock Inc.; p.28 © Masahito Mori / © rui vale sousa/ Shutterstock Inc.; p.29 © abd/ Shutterstock Inc.; p.30 © Hasan Shaheed/ Shutterstock Inc.; p.31 © Piotr Marcinski/ Shutterstock Inc.; p.32 © Lisa S./ Shutterstock Inc.; p.33 © Cheryl Casey/ Shutterstock Inc.; p.34 © Tracy Whiteside/ Shutterstock Inc.; p.35 © hartphotography / Shutterstock Inc.; p.36 © Jorg Hackemann/ Shutterstock Inc.; p.37 © Jaimie Duplass/ Shutterstock Inc.; p.38 © Alexander Gitlits/ Shutterstock Inc.; p.39 © O Driscoll Imaging/ Shutterstock Inc.; p.40 © auremar/ Shutterstock Inc.; p.41 © cate_89/ Shutterstock Inc.; p.43 © Lisa F.Young/ Shutterstock Inc.; p.45 © AISPIX by Image Source / Shutterstock Inc.; torn paper background © Leksus Tuss; banners: © Amgun/ Shutterstock Inc.

Library and Archives Canada Cataloguing in Publication

Webb, Margaret, 1962-
      Social bullying / Margaret Webb.

(Take a stand against bullying)
Includes index.
Issued also in electronic format.
ISBN 978-0-7787-7915-5 (bound).--ISBN 978-0-7787-7920-9 (pbk.)

      1. Libel and slander--Juvenile literature. 2. Social isolation--Juvenile literature. 3. Bullying--Juvenile literature. I. Title.
II. Series: Take a stand against bullying

BJ1535.S6W43 2013   j302.5'45   C2013-900256-1

Library of Congress Cataloging-in-Publication Data

Webb, Margaret, 1962-
   Social bullying / Margaret Webb.
      pages cm. -- (Take a stand against bullying)
   Includes index.
   ISBN 978-0-7787-7915-5 (reinforced library binding) -- ISBN 978-0-7787-7920-9 (pbk.) -- ISBN 978-1-4271-9076-5 (electronic pdf) -- ISBN 978-1-4271-9130-4 (electronic html)
   1. Interpersonal relations in children--Juvenile literature. 2. Social interaction in children--Juvenile literature. 3. Social isolation--Juvenile literature. 4. Bullying--Prevention--Juvenile literature. I. Title.

BF723.I646W43 2013
302.34'3--dc23
                                    2013000583

Crabtree Publishing Company

www.crabtreebooks.com   1-800-387-7650

Printed in Canada/022013/BF20130114

Published in Canada
Crabtree Publishing
616 Welland Ave.
St. Catharines, ON
L2M 5V6

Published in the United States
Crabtree Publishing
PMB 59051
350 Fifth Avenue, 59th Floor
New York, NY 10118

Published in the United Kingdom
Crabtree Publishing
Maritime House
Basin Road North, Hove
BN41 1WR

Published in Australia
Crabtree Publishing
3 Charles Street
Coburg North
VIC, 3058

CONTENTS

"Come hang with us!"

Me? thought Kate.

The five girls calling to her were the most popular in grade six. At least, that's how they always acted, like they were cooler than everyone else. Today, they clumped together in the school yard, rating what girls the boys liked best.

Kate couldn't believe they wanted her to be part of their group. On the very first day in art class, the five girls told her how much they liked her painting. Then they invited her to have lunch with them.

Kate smiled and walked over to the girls. But when she reached them, they turned their backs. She heard them giggling, saying that no boy would ever like Kate because she was a total loser. Then they turned around and shouted, "Hi!" as if they weren't even talking about her.

Kate felt like she had been punched in the stomach. She never knew if her friends were going to be mean or nice to her. But Kate didn't think the girls were **bullying** her because they never hit her or teased her directly, like other bullies had last year. And they were her new friends! Her only friends.

She began thinking they were right. No boy would ever like her unless she hung around with the popular girls and learned to act like them. Except the girls found something wrong with everything Kate did. She felt hopeless. She started hating everything about herself.

In art class, when the teacher asked them to draw a self-portrait, the five girls looked at Kate and started giggling. Kate felt sick to her stomach. She knew she could never make herself beautiful.

4

INTRODUCTION
The Nature of Bullying

Kate may not realize it, but she is being bullied. This type of **bullying** is called **social bullying**, and it goes way beyond good-natured teasing. The bullies want to make their **targets** feel bad about themselves.

Social bullying involves name-calling, verbal insults, and excluding someone from a group. It is more subtle than **physical bullying**, which involves physical aggression and violence. But social bullying is serious. It can be very harmful not only to the targets, but also to the bullies and the bystanders who watch. Doing nothing to stop such bullying creates an environment where people say mean things to each other, spread nasty rumors, and exclude kids from social groups. One day, you might be the bully or the bystander, but the next day everything might turn around and you may be the victim! No one can feel safe.

In this book, you will learn about the different kinds of social bullying. You will learn why kids do it, how it is harmful, and why it is important to stop it.

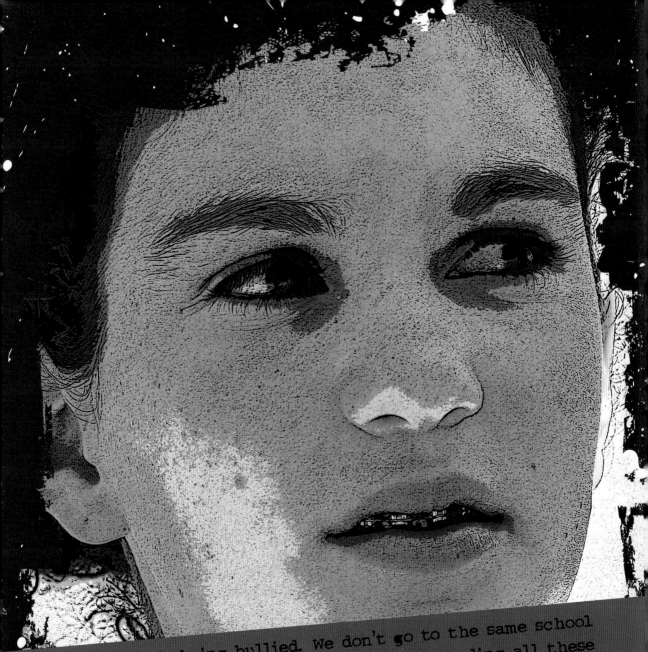

"My friend is being bullied. We don't go to the same school so I can't hang out with her. Girls are spreading all these bad rumors about her on the Internet. I read them and I know they're not true. Now my friend's getting this really bad reputation and no one likes her. She's really sad. She has no one to hang out with. I don't know how to help her." Jessie, age 13

CHAPTER 1
What is Social Bullying?

Social bullying is a term that covers a range of harmful acts. The bully has more social power—more friends or status with friends—and uses that power to hurt, embarrass, ridicule, or threaten someone with less social power. The attacks are unprovoked and repeated against the same person. Kids social bully other kids in a number of ways. They might gossip about someone, spread false and hurtful rumors, write mean notes or graffiti, or make **menacing** and negative facial gestures to cause fear or shame.

Social bullying is also making nasty jokes or playing pranks to **humiliate** someone. It can also be excluding someone or intentionally forcing someone out of a social group. The target loses friends and feels alone, ashamed, and fearful.

What's So Bad About Cyber Bullying?

Spreading lies or posting embarrassing pictures of someone online allows a bully to remain **anonymous**. The target of the attack often has no idea who is tormenting them. The **anonymity** makes it more likely for other kids to participate in the bullying by reposting the offensive comment or picture. The target ends up feeling like the entire world is against him or her.

Behind One's Back

Social bullying is often indirect. The bully might spread nasty lies behind a victim's back or write offensive graffiti about someone, making it difficult to confront the bully or even know where the lies are coming from. Now, many of these bullying tactics are carried out anonymously on the Internet through **social media**, texting, and other technologies. This form of social bullying is called **cyber bullying**, and it can be even more harmful.

?Did You Know?

Girls are more likely than boys to target a friend and try to exclude that girl from a social group. Tween girls, between ages 9 and 13, are most likely to engage in this mean behavior.

Where Does Social Bullying Happen?

Most social bullying happens at school, often at recess, when there is little organized activity or supervision. But bullying can happen anywhere kids gather: after-school programs, sports events, community and church groups, on the Internet, and even at home among families.

In fact, kids often learn bullying behavior from older siblings and parents who may behave aggressively in their relationships.

How Common is Social Bullying?

Social bullying is very common. Experts say the activity starts in the earliest grades, with name-calling and teasing. If this behavior goes unchecked, social bullying becomes widespread in schools. Experts say that in a class of 35 students, between four and six children are involved in bullying behavior, either bullying others or being bullied.

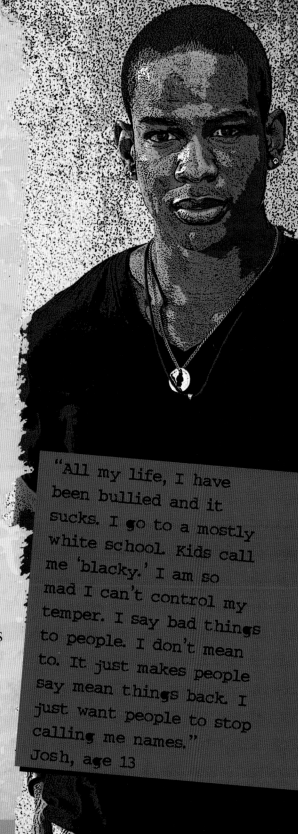

"All my life, I have been bullied and it sucks. I go to a mostly white school. Kids call me 'blacky.' I am so mad I can't control my temper. I say bad things to people. I don't mean to. It just makes people say mean things back. I just want people to stop calling me names."
Josh, age 13

Who is Likely to Be a Social Bully?

Kids who bully may be victims of bullying themselves. They may have learned the behavior from parents who behave aggressively with each other and their children. They may be tormented by older siblings. They may have friends who bully and they join in to avoid being bullied themselves.

But social bullies are often just regular kids. They may not recognize their behavior as bullying. These kids may be well-adjusted, have a lot of friends, do well in school, and act respectively toward authority figures, such as teachers and parents.

What is Relational Aggression?

Relational aggression is a form of social bullying common among tweens (ages 9 to 13), especially tween girls. A bully may act alone or, more often, with friends. The target of aggression is usually a friend within their group. Think of the term "frenemies" from the movie *Mean Girls*, and you get an idea of how social bullies behave.

The aggressors start picking on someone in the group of friends, either to control, put down, or push that person out of the group. This type of bullying can hurt even more because it comes from people you think are your friends. It's more difficult to escape because the target may have to give up friends.

Who is Involved?

A bully might be physically bigger or have more social power. They might belong to the cool group or have a lot of friends. They bully to gain more social power. They put other people down and hope to look good by comparison.

The target of bullying is the **victim**. They may be physically smaller, younger, or have less social standing within a group.

Bystanders are those who **witness** the bullying. There are two types of bystanders: those who watch and take no action and those who take action by trying to stop the bullying or by reporting it to an authority who can stop it.

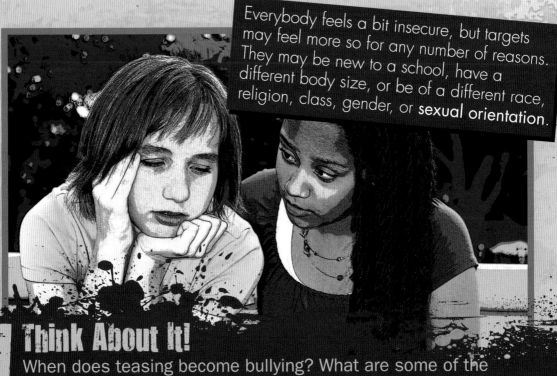

Everybody feels a bit insecure, but targets may feel more so for any number of reasons. They may be new to a school, have a different body size, or be of a different race, religion, class, gender, or **sexual orientation.**

! Think About It!

When does teasing become bullying? What are some of the insults or nasty lies that kids use to humiliate other students at your school? Lots of kids—and even adults—spread nasty gossip about other people. Why do we do it?

"Some girls don't get how to be popular. So I tell them what to wear and how to act. If a girl doesn't do what I say, I'll make something up about her, like she's a whore or something. When everyone starts calling her that, she usually starts dressing the way I tell her. If someone's going to hang around me, I don't want them embarrassing me." Chloe, age 14

CHAPTER 2
Why Gossiping Hurts

Behavior that is **widespread** can seem pretty normal: gossiping behind someone's back, posting a hurtful comment about someone on Facebook, or telling a big lie, like the straight-A student cheated on a test when you have no proof.

Kids spread **malicious gossip** and lies to impress their friends, as pay back for something nasty someone said about them, to get laughs, to feel better about their own insecurities, or to hurt someone because they just don't like them. Gossiping negatively about other kids and spreading nasty and malicious rumors and lies is social bullying. It is not funny or normal behavior and can be extremely damaging and dangerous.

When you take part in it, you are helping to create an environment where social bullying becomes widespread and normal. No one is safe in that kind of environment. One day, you may be spreading malicious gossip about someone at school and the next day other people could be saying nasty things about you. We all have a right to learn and play in safe environments. Kids should not have to worry or be stressed out that someone is spreading malicious gossip and lies to hurt them.

What is Malicious Gossip?

- You know something about a friend or classmate that you know will hurt that person if you tell others or make it public by posting it on social media. But you do it anyway.

- You tell a lie about someone or repeat a lie that hurts that person's reputation and may cause them to lose friends.

- You exaggerate an event or situation even though you know it will hurt the reputations of the people involved.

- You say or repeat something about someone that you know is untrue in order to put that person down.

- You pass notes in class or post things on the Internet that may be hurtful or damaging to someone's reputation.

Why Do Kids Spread Malicious Gossip?

Social bullies spread rumors and lies about someone to destroy that person's reputation within a school or group of friends, or exclude that person from a social group. They may even do it to manipulate someone into doing something to avoid the lies or secrets being spread about them.

Some kids take part in this behavior because it seems like all the other kids are doing it. But spreading nasty lies and rumors hurts people, destroys reputations, and can turn friends against each other.

"I thought this girl was my best friend so I told her stuff. She told my friends I was telling everyone their secrets. Now they don't want to hang out with me. This girl pretends to be my friend on Facebook, but she's always telling me stuff she's doing with her new friends —my old friends!—like going to movies. But they never invite me anymore. I probably deserve everything I'm getting. I feel really stupid and embarrassed. And no one likes me. I just feel like disappearing." Jasmyne, age 13

How to Stand Up to Malicious Gossip

Tell the gossipers that spreading lies about you or anyone else is definitely not cool. Don't return the bad behavior by spreading malicious gossip about them. That will only lead to more bullying.

Try talking to someone who can help—such as friends, teachers, parents, school administrators, counselors, or anonymous phone helplines.

Adults used to tell kids to "laugh it off" or ignore someone who is teasing them. That's still true some of the time, but when it comes to malicious gossip and other kinds of bullying, playing it cool is not the best option.

Lasting Damage

Kids who are shamed by malicious gossip experience lasting damage. Bullying causes stress, anxiety, and fear. Targets might have trouble concentrating at school or may try to avoid school altogether. Targets are more likely to drop out of school. Adults who were bullied as kids have lower self-esteem and suffer higher rates of depression. Sometimes kids who are bullied feel so helpless and depressed that they think about suicide, and some even act on those thoughts.

? Did You Know?

Spreading malicious gossip hurts bullies, too. Kids will quickly learn not to trust bullies and the bullies will eventually lose their friends.

How Can We All Stop Malicious Gossiping?

If you hear bullies spreading malicious gossip and do nothing—or worse—pass it on, you are part of the problem. If you allow this harmful behavior to continue, one day it might hurt you.

Get active on this issue. Stop spreading gossip. Get your teacher to discuss why malicious gossiping is bad. Talk to your friends about how spreading hurtful rumors creates a bad atmosphere for everyone and make a pact with them to stop rumors before they start.

Support the kids being targeted by inviting them to hang out with you so they feel less alone.

Think About It!

Have you ever felt pressured by a friend to act or dress in a new way? Do you ever think someone deserves to be teased? Do girls gossip about different stuff than boys? How so?

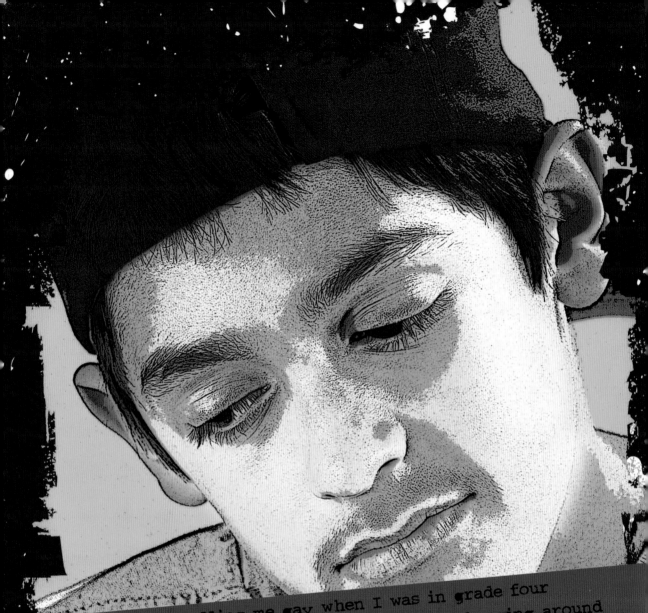

"Guys started calling me gay when I was in grade four because my best friend was a girl. I stopped hanging around with her. Now I'm in grade six and they still make all these jokes. No one wants to sit next to me in the changeroom at hockey. I just ignored them. But now there's this new guy who sticks up for me. He wants to be my friend. But I don't want to be friends. I know everyone will just call him my boyfriend. I can't be friends with anybody. I really can't take this. I love hockey, but I don't want to play anymore."

Richard, age 12

CHAPTER 3
Bullies Make Social Outcasts

Everyone is different. Those differences are what make each of us special and unique. Social bullies do not celebrate differences. Instead, they use these differences to exclude someone from groups of friends, teammates, classmates, or other social groups. A social bully's message is usually "You're different, you don't belong, get out." The target ultimately feels like a **social outcast**.

This kind of bullying usually takes place at school and wherever else kids gather. A lot of bullying is done using social media. One survey found that 65 percent of kids admitted to being cyber bullied. Of those who witnessed a bullying incident, between 80 and 90 percent said that it made them feel uncomfortable. They felt they should step in to help, but often didn't know how.

Everyone is Different

Bullies pick on kids who look different, such as kids who are heavier, skinnier, taller, or have ears that stick out. They tease kids who have different backgrounds—either richer or poorer, or from another culture, country, religion, or race. They taunt kids with different abilities, such as learning or physical challenges. They torment kids who act differently. Often kids whose interests differ from those of the most "popular" kids can become the target of bullying. Kids who don't match our old-fashioned ideas about gender—such as boys who like art and dance and girls who play rough sports—are often the victims of a bully at some point in their lives.

? Did You Know?

Everyone is unique, with their own qualities, talents, and faults. And you will find, as you get older, that being different is what makes you cool and interesting! Some of the most successful people in the world were picked on for being different when they were young.

Bullies are often insecure. By tormenting someone for their differences, bullies attempt to make that person feel more insecure. By comparison, the bully feels more powerful, more popular, and more in control of the social group. The goal of bullying is to take someone else's power to build up your own.

The Long-Term Damage

Victims are pushed out of their social group or choose to leave the group. They are made to feel like social outcasts. Losing a social group causes deep distress, anxiety, and depression in victims. When someone feels very alone, he or she might have thoughts of suicide. Tragically, some victims of social bullying do act on these feelings and end their lives.

Bullies suffer too. Unless they learn to change their behavior, they will continue to bully as a way of gaining power over people rather than seeking more positive ways to feel good about themselves. As adults, they may have difficulty maintaining healthy relationships at work and with friends and family.

Allowing bullying to persist hurts us all.

Bullying and Homophobia

A study found that anti-gay slurs such as "homo," "faggot," and "sissy" are the most heard insults in school. These derogatory comments are directed toward kids who are or are perceived to be lesbian, gay, bisexual, or transgender (LGBT). Having a negative attitude and feelings toward homosexuality is called **homophobia**. Homophobic bullying may include malicious name-calling, spreading rumors, or gossiping that someone is gay, as well as excluding and isolating them.

Many schools have gay–straight alliances, which are support groups whose purpose is to lend support to LGBT students as well as working to make the school safe for all.

"There's this boy in my class and he's gay. He only told me because I'm one of the only accepting people in our school. But my guy friends are really mean to him. I tell them to stop and it makes me furious, but they just keep going. They wrote in big letters, 'Robert is a FAG!' on his locker. He's getting really upset and he has already attempted suicide. What can I do?" Jacob, age 14

Gossipers Don't Win

Long-term, malicious gossipers definitely do not win. When other kids hear you gossiping they will be suspicious about what you might say about them. People will not be able to trust you. It may become hard to make and keep friends. If you spread rumors and malicious gossip you may feel remorse for your actions when you see how they hurt the target.

Gender Differences

Experts say that social bullying over gender differences starts as early as grade two, with kids taunting boys and girls that do not fall into strict **gender stereotypes**. Boys that are shy, sensitive, artistic, musical, nonathletic, or honor students are bullied because these traits are not considered masculine. Girls can be bullied for being athletic, unattractive, or unstylish dressers, or for enjoying typically masculine pursuits. It is wrong to use gender stereotypes to judge other people. Everyone should be free to wear what they want, like what they like, and not be bullied for it.

Think About It!

Have your friends ever tried to push someone out of your group? What did you do? Why does calling someone gay hurt everyone? Think of something you love doing. How would you feel if kids made you stop doing it?

"My friends and I started teasing this girl. She was really nerdy and gross. So we just started insulting her, calling her 'lezzie' and 'dyke.' She didn't look like a lezzie or anything. We just wanted to keep her away from us. She ended up trying to kill herself. I feel really bad about what we did. We were so stupid. I wish someone had made us stop." Madison, age 14

CHAPTER 4
Why Insults Hurt

It's natural for kids to playfully tease each other, but many kids don't know the difference between playful teasing and bullying. Teasing is about having fun and building friendships. But insulting kids to make them feel bad or look stupid in front of other people is bullying. Spreading nasty rumors, threatening gestures, nasty pranks, and mean jokes—with the goal of trying to scare, shame, or ridicule someone—is bullying.

If kids respond positively to your teasing— if they laugh or want to play along—then chances are you are teasing in a good-natured way. If kids respond negatively—if they want you to stop or get upset or respond by trying to insult you back—then your teasing has crossed the line into bullying. The best thing to do is stop and apologize.

The Impact of Insults

Bullies want to destroy the self-esteem of their victims. They want to make other kids feel insecure and bad about themselves. This is why bullying is so harmful. After listening to the insults, victims may start to believe that there is something wrong with them and that they deserve to be bullied. They start to feel alone and insecure. These feelings make it even harder to stand up to bullies or to report bullying to an adult who can help stop it.

"This guy was always teasing this girl for having big teeth. My friends and I thought it was pretty funny. Then I saw the girl was getting really upset. I just snapped one day. I said, 'You know what? It's not funny anymore.' I told the guys to leave her alone. And they did." Cameron, age 13

Did You Know? ?

Bullying is the fourth most common reason young people seek help from hotline and helpline services for kids.

Everyone Deserves Respect

If someone is bullying you, try to remember the most important thing: you don't deserve it and it's not your fault! No one deserves to be bullied by anyone. It is the bully who is at fault.

What's wrong is the bullying, not you or anything about you.

Everyone has the right to safety and respectful treatment. Adults and kids need to work together to stop bullying and protect those rights.

Work together with adults and kids to stop bullying. Trying to stand up to bullies without support is a hard thing to do.

Report Bullying!

Kids have a code: don't tattle, don't snitch, don't tell, and don't rat each other out to adults. There is a difference between being a tattletale and reporting dangerous bullying behavior. But sometimes it's hard for kids to know the difference. Bullies exploit that by threatening to make things worse if victims "tell." And it takes a great deal of courage to step forward and report bullying, whether it's as a victim or a bystander.

Therefore, it's important for teachers, counselors, coaches, parents, and guardians to take bullying seriously and address the behavior, and perhaps the circumstances that lead to it, in a compassionate and thoughtful way. Without intervention, bullying can quickly progress from nasty verbal insults to physical violence.

How to Stop Insults

If you are the target of bullying, insulting the person back will just make the situation worse. Be assertive. Tell the bully to stop, but don't fight back with taunts of your own.

Try to stay calm and look confident. Remember, the bully is trying to make you look or feel bad. If you look strong, like the insults don't hurt you, you are showing that the attack isn't working. Chances are the bully will lose interest in taunting you.

Walking away and ignoring a bully might work in some situations, but if it doesn't you should take further action. Go to an area away from the bully or hang out with friends who support you. Talk to your friends about ways to deal with the bullying. Allowing insults and nasty pestering to persist creates a negative and nasty atmosphere for everyone.

If you and your friends can't stop the taunts on your own, speak to an adult. Talking about what you are going through helps. Tell an adult you trust about how the bullying hurts you and ask them to help you deal with the situation.

If you're afraid to speak up, write an anonymous note to an adult to explain what's going on. Call a kids help phone line and get help from a counselor.

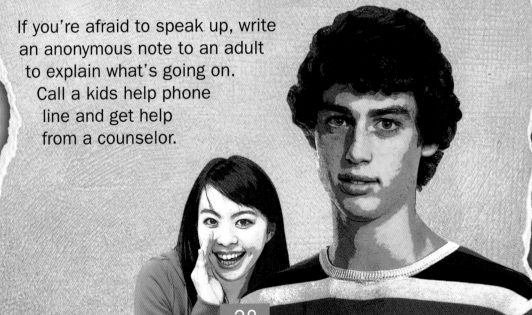

What if an Adult Doesn't Help?

It can be tough to stop bullies. Bullies can be popular with friends and even teachers and coaches. They might get good grades, do well in school, and be good at sports. If you tell an adult that someone like that is bullying you, he or she may not want to believe it.

If that happens, it can be very hurtful. But don't give up! Talk to another adult, perhaps someone who doesn't know the bully very well. Take a friend with you for support. Gather other kids who have been insulted and report the bullying as a group.

"People started picking on me when I got really bad acne. It's bad enough without everyone constantly calling me 'zit face' I don't want to go to school or be around anyone. My parents say it will go away, but I don't think I can wait."
Sofia, age 14

▌ Think About It!

When does teasing become bullying? How can friends work together to stop bullying? How can adults help?

"I hate it when boys say stuff about girls, like calling them dirty names. I want to tell them to stop, but if I do they start calling me a lesbian, like I stick up for girls because I love them. I know they're just stupid but it really makes me mad." Aaliyah, age 13

CHAPTER 5
Understanding Power Players

Social bullying can often be overlooked as normal group dynamics among young people. Many adults think some behaviors are just part of growing up. But we know now that social bullying isn't normal—it causes real and lasting harm.

Kids who become targets of social bullies already seem weaker in some way. Social bullies are very good at identifying and taking advantage of any perceived weakness. And while verbal and physical bullying happen in the moment and are easy to recognize, social bullying has a different dynamic. Acts of social bullying can often seem like no big deal to someone on the outside.

But, social bullying causes lasting damage. Regardless of why victims are targeted, social bullying will lead to insecurity and can destroy victims' confidence and self-esteem. Victims may also lose friends and feel misunderstood and alone. They may develop a negative attitude toward school, relationships, and society.

How Do You Know if You Are a Bully?

You are bullying when you try to hurt or ridicule a person by verbally insulting them, or if you try to make that person feel unwanted and unliked in some way.

You are bullying when you target the same victim or victims over and over.

You are bullying if you use your social power in negative ways to pick on someone you think is weaker, has fewer friends, or is vulnerable in some way.

If someone calls you a bully or you feel like a bully after an incident, chances are that you are bullying.

Understanding the Bully

All kids want social power, including friends, attention, and respect. Some kids seek social power in positive ways. They are kind and supportive friends, fun to be around, and do well in school and other activities. Other kids try to get social power in negative ways. They take power from kids they perceive to be weaker. They begin name-calling and insulting others. This social bullying can feel good because the bully feels more powerful than the person being picked on. The more attention bullies get for this behavior (e.g. by others laughing at the taunts), the more powerful they feel and the more they will continue. They may **escalate** their attacks and target more victims, creating a negative, unsafe environment for everyone.

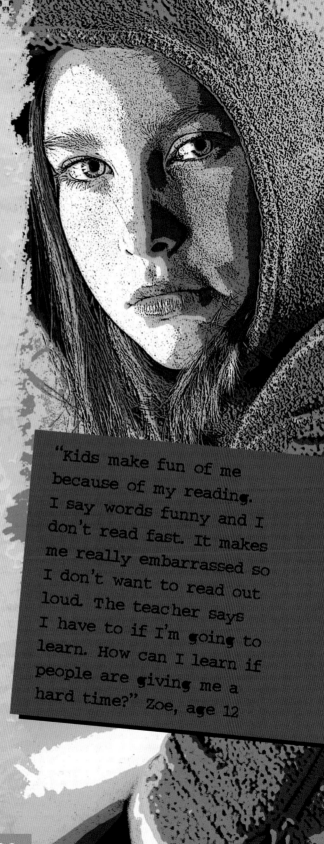

Long-Lasting Damages

Kids who bully, who learn to get social power through intimidation and fear, suffer long-lasting damage. A bully may be respected out of fear, but a bully is rarely well-liked.

If their behavior is not stopped and corrected, they will have difficulty developing positive relationship skills. Bullies will have trouble relating well to others at school and work, or forming close friendships and romantic relationships. A bully is more likely to drop out of school, abuse drugs and alcohol, and serve time in jail.

? Did You Know?

One study showed that 60 percent of kids who were identified as bullies between grades six and eight had a criminal record by the time they were 24 years old.

"Kids make fun of me because of my reading. I say words funny and I don't read fast. It makes me really embarrassed so I don't want to read out loud. The teacher says I have to if I'm going to learn. How can I learn if people are giving me a hard time?" Zoe, age 12

Why It's Tough to Act

Acting against bullying takes courage. Bystanders often don't know what to do or they are afraid the bullies will turn on them. Acting against social bullying is especially difficult because it's very likely that the bystanders are the bully's friends.

Anyone can be the target of social bullying. If you don't take a stand, nobody wins. Social bullying creates an environment where being mean is normal, and that's not good for anyone—not the targets, the bullies, or the bystanders.

There are many ways to act. You can set an example—make an effort to be nice to the target. Show the bully that being mean isn't cool with you. And if you are afraid to stand up in public, you can take more indirect action. If your friend is a bully, tell him or her that you have more interesting ways to spend your time than tormenting your classmates.

You can also support the target of a bully privately—tell them that what the bully is doing is wrong and offer to go with them to report the incident to an adult. Even if you afraid of standing up to the bully yourself, supporting the victim in private might be just what he or she needs to take action.

You may feel powerless to act, but remember that most of your peers want bullying to stop, too. Seek out friends who feel like you do and together you can create a safe environment for everyone.

Understanding the Bystander

Almost all kids witness verbal and social bullying because it is so widespread. Although not directly involved like the bully or victim, bystanders actually play an extremely important role, even if they do not realize it.

Hurtful Bystanders

If bystanders see someone being insulted and do nothing, or worse, laugh or jeer at the victim, they are encouraging the bully. They become hurtful bystanders who contribute to the bullying.

Helpful Bystanders

Bystanders can stop or **neutralize** the effects of social bullying in a number of ways. They can tell the bullies to stop, that insulting someone is not cool. They can support the victim by offering friendship, telling the victim to ignore the insults, and taking the victim away from the bully. They can also get other bystanders to help by discouraging the bully and supporting the victim. Then they can report the bullying to an adult.

! Think About It!

If you witness social bullying, what are ways you can be a helpful bystander? Kids insulting and calling each other names is widespread in many schools. What have you said that has been hurtful to someone and how do you think it made them feel? How do you feel now that you know you may have socially bullied someone?

"Things used to be really bad at our school. People would insult each other and call each other names. Then they started teaching about bullying in the classrooms. Kids started realizing some of the stuff they were doing was really mean. We learned how to stick up for each other. Now when someone starts calling people names, we just all say, 'You know what? It's not cool.' The person usually stops. It really changed things. I like school a lot more now." Sam, age 12

CHAPTER 6
It Takes a Group Effort

Preventing social bullying requires a group effort.

Targets of bullying should not be made to feel like they have to stand up to the bully alone or put up with the abuse. They need help from other students, teachers, and their families.

If no one **intervenes** to stop social bullying, the bully gains supporters and social power, and targets more victims. That provokes other kids to seek social power in this negative way, making social bullying widespread.

The most effective way to keep social bullying from becoming prevalent is to stop bullying as soon as it occurs and support the victim. Everyone—kids, teachers, school administrators, and families— must work together to recognize social bullying and develop strategies to prevent it.

The Whole-School Approach

Experts believe a "whole-school" approach is the most effective way to prevent bullying. Both educators and students must be involved in creating an antibullying program. As well, everyone must work together to enforce it.

Student's Role

Students contribute valuable ideas to programs because they know first-hand how bullying works and what is effective discipline. Kids can often suggest situations and locations where more adult supervision could prevent bullying. They also want to learn skills to deal with social bullying.

"Kids are always calling stuff that's lame or stupid 'gay.' I did it in front of my aunt, who's gay. She looked shocked. I felt bad because my aunt's really cool and I didn't mean to hurt her. It made me realize I could be hurting all kinds of people by saying stuff's gay when I mean it's stupid. So I don't use it anymore." Mia, age 11

? Did You Know?

When asked, most kids want earlier intervention by teachers and more effective consequences for those who bully.

School's Role

Effective whole-school approaches have strong educational components that teach kids how to recognize social bullying and empowers them to become helpful bystanders. Students learn strategies to spot, stop, and report bullying and also ways to support victims.

Class-based discussions can also help those who social bully change their negative behavior. They can, for instance, learn to get friends and attention through positive leadership and by supporting more vulnerable classmates rather than teasing them.

For these programs to be effective, teachers and school authorities must be committed to enforcing them. They must act on students' complaints of social bullying by following through with effective discipline for the bully and support for the victim.

Victims need help recovering their confidence and finding ways back into social groups that excluded them.

A Successful Approach

Insults and name-calling can be so widespread in schools, even teachers can be overwhelmed. That was the case in one city elementary school. Teachers had little hope of changing the behavior of students.

The school called in an antibullying counselor to help develop a strategy. The counselor asked the teachers to identify one insult that was most prevalent. Teachers agreed that students used the term "you're gay" or "that's so gay" in negative and hurtful ways, yet did not take it seriously.

The counselor worked with the teachers to develop a plan to eliminate the use of those phrases on school grounds. Teachers doubted it could be done, but they gave it a try. They developed lesson plans to explain to students why the term was hurtful. They taught students that the proper way to deal with anger at someone or a situation is to simply state they are upset and explain why, rather than resorting to name-calling. Whenever teachers heard students using the term, they acted on every instance and reminded students about the lesson.

Students joined the effort and, by the end of the year, they had stopped using the hurtful term.

The teachers were so encouraged by the success, they were ready to work with students on developing a broader, whole-school antibullying program.

Family's Role

Parents and families play an important role—they can empower kids to stand up to bullies as both targets and bystanders. But they should also act on complaints about social bullying by reporting incidents and getting help for their kids. Families of reported bullies must also be part of the solution by supporting discipline strategies and helping their child understand why bullying is wrong.

? Did You Know?

There is a growing movement in schools called "Nice it Forward." Students use social media to send positive messages and support to other students. These campaigns encourage everyone to be nice to each other.

To create a safe and inclusive environment free of bullying, students, teachers, school authorities, and families must all work together.

! Think About It!

Why is using the term "you're so gay" hurtful to all of us? What insults are widely used in your school? What could you do to help

CHAPTER 7
Empowering Yourself:
What You Can Do if You Are Being Bullied

If you are being bullied, try to take some comfort in the fact that you are not alone. One study found that 88 percent of kids in junior high school had witnessed bullying, and one in four students admitted to being bullied. Bullying is all around us. If you become a target, here are some things you can do to protect yourself.

Learn to spot the bullies

Some bullies like to threaten and intimidate others with their size, take other people's stuff, and say insulting things. Other bullies like to spread malicious gossip and lies, control friends by telling them how to think about other people, or put other kids down.

Stay away from these bullies

Avoid being alone with them. Stick close to friends for support, sit close to the driver on a school bus, and stay near teachers at breaks or when changing classes. Don't make yourself a target by bringing money or expensive things to school.

Stay calm

When you're being targeted, try to stay calm. It's normal to be upset and even cry, but bullies are looking for that reaction. If you can stay calm in front of the bully, he or she may lose interest. Try and wait until you're in a safe place to release your emotions.

Act confident

Bullies tend to target kids who lack confidence or assertiveness. Even if you are afraid, keep your head up and speak in a firm voice. But don't fight back, either verbally or physically. That will only make the bullying worse. Don't plan revenge on the bully. That will only encourage the bully and cause the bullying to continue.

Talk to the bully

Tell the bully to stop bothering you. Explain why the behavior bothers you and why it's not cool. Don't give into the bully's demands to do something you don't want to do.

Walk away

Sometimes you can't get a bully to listen to reason or stop insulting you, but walking away will usually end the incident.

Talk to an adult who can help

This is critical, especially if a bully is targeting you repeatedly. Everyone has a right to be respected and safe. By reporting bullying, you will save yourself and others from these damaging attacks and create a safer environment for everyone.

Don't feel as if you deserve to be bullied.

The bully is the one with the problem, not you. If you let the bully make you feel bad about yourself, then the bully is winning.

Remember, what's wrong is their behavior, not you.

Are You a Social Bully?

One in five kids admit to bullying others. It takes courage to admit to negative behavior. Chances are the number of kids who social bully is much higher. Probably most people have done something at some point that might be considered social bullying. Take this quiz to find out if you have, and also find out how you can change that behavior.

1. Do you ever try to make people feel left out?

2. Do you ever spread rumors or gossip, even if you don't know if it's true?

3. Do you ever laugh when someone is being teased in a way that clearly hurts them?

4. When you're upset with someone, do you speak negatively to your friends about that person?

5. Do you ever try to convince your friends not to like someone you don't like?

6. Do you ever make fun of people's appearance, clothes, or the way they act?

7. Do you ever threaten someone to make them behave in a certain way or to do something you want?

8. Do you ever harass girls by calling them sexual names?

9. Do you ever use the term "that's so gay" or call people gay?

10. Do you ever write mean things about people or post embarrassing pictures of others on the Internet?

If you answered "yes" to any question—and almost everyone will to one—you have participated in social bullying. If you answered "yes" to more than three questions, you may be on your way to becoming a social bully.

How to Change Your Behavior

- If you stop gossiping, friends will trust you more.
- If you're upset with someone, talk to them directly.
- Improve your own self-esteem by being a better friend.
- Being inclusive and making others feel welcome is the best way to make friends.
- Become a positive leader by standing up to bullying and supporting victims.
- Earn respect from your peers by sticking up for people rather than teasing them.
- Try to understand and value differences, rather than using them against your peers.
- Think about how you would feel if a person with more power bullied you.

Learning how to recognize and stop social bullying will help create a safe, positive, and bully-free environment for everybody.

Other Resources

Bullying is a big, difficult, and sometimes scary issue, but you don't have to face it alone—as a target, bystander, or bully. You can get help dealing with your situation. There are many phone hotlines with trained counselors who can offer advice and support and you don't have to tell anyone your name. There are also websites, organizations, and books that offer great information.

Books

The Reluctant Journal of Henry K. Larsen by Susin Nielsen (Tundra Books, 2012)

Bullies, Bigmouths, and So-Called Friends by Jenny Alexander (Hodder Children's Books, 2006)

Mean Chicks, Cliques, and Dirty Tricks: A Real Girl's Guide to Getting Through the Day With Smarts and Style by V. Shearin Karres (Adams Media Corporation, 2004)

Websites

It Gets Better Project
www.itgetsbetter.org

This online project shows young LGBT (lesbian, gay, bisexual, and transgendered) kids that they can be happy, find love, and live great lives. The site also has great tips on how to deal with bullying.

www.bullying.org

This site aims to stop bullying through education and awareness. You will find great tips and information.

www.stopcyberbullying.org

Brought to kids by a network of antibullying experts, this was the first cyber bullying prevention program in North America. The website is filled with information about cyber bullying and how to deal with it.

PREVNet: Promoting Relationships and Eliminating Violence Network
www.prevnet.ca

This is an organization created by researchers, governments, teachers, and other groups committed to stop bullying. This is a good website written by professionals with a lot of great information, not just for kids, but also for parents, teachers, and researchers.

Organizations, Hotlines, and Helplines

Boys Town National Hotline (United States) (1-800-448-3000)
www.yourlifeyourvoice.org

Both boys and girls can call this free national hotline to talk to a counselor about anything at anytime.

Kids Help Phone (Canada) (1-800-668-6868)
www.kidshelpphone.ca

Counselors offer anonymous and free confidential support, 24 hours a day, seven days a week.

STOMP Out Bullying Help Line (United States) (855-790-4357)
www.stompoutbullying.org/livechat_portal.php

This live help chat line is free and confidential for kids over age 13 with issues of being bullied, cyber bullied, or at risk of suicide.

The National Suicide Prevention Lifeline (United States) (800-273-8255)
www.suicidepreventionlifeline.org

Feeling really sad or like you might hurt yourself? For kids in crisis in the United States, you can call this hotline 24 hours a day, 7 days a week, and you will be put in touch with a trained counselor at a crisis center in your area.

My Gay Straight Alliance (Canada) (www.mygsa.ca)
MGSA.ca is Canada's website for safer and inclusive schools for the lesbian, gay, bisexual, trans, queer, and questioning (LGBTQ) community.

The Trevor Project (United States) (866-488-7386)
www.thetrevorproject.org

This organization provides crisis intervention and suicide prevention services to lesbian, gay, bisexual, transgender, and questioning youth.

Glossary

anonymity The state of being unknown

anonymous Not named or identified

bullying Repeated, aggressive behavior intended to hurt and to gain power over the victim

bystander A person who is present at an incident but does not take part

cyber bullying Using technology (email, texts, blogs, social networking sites) to intimidate a person, hurt their feelings, or damage their reputation

escalate To increase in intensity

gender stereotype An idea about the way men or women are "supposed" to act or dress

homophobia Thinking less of people who are gay or lesbian

humiliate Making someone feel intense embarrassment

intervene To come between in order to stop a dispute

malicious gossip Gossip that is intended to harm a person

menacing A threatening or dangerous manner

neutralize To make ineffective

physical bullying Hitting, punching, kicking, slapping, or any other act of physical violence

relational aggression A type of psychological abuse in which harm is caused through or to relationships

sexual orientation Identity based on whether a person is attracted to the same sex (homosexual), the opposite sex (heterosexual), or both sexes (bisexual)

social bullying Intentionally damaging someone's social life/relationships by excluding someone from a group on purpose, spreading rumors, or telling others to avoid that person (also known as relational bullying)

social media Online communities in which users share information, ideas, personal messages, and other content

social outcast A person who is rejected or in some way excluded from society

target The person selected as the aim of an attack

victim A person harmed by another

widespread Found over a wide area, accepted by many people

witness A person who sees something happen

Index